Book 1

Harpsicle® Harp Method

by Darlene Walton

Online Video

Video
dv.melbay.com/22020
You Tube
www.melbay.com/22020V

Video Chapters

1	Introduction	7	Hands and Fingers
2	About the Harpsicle® Harp	8	Chords and Arpeggios
3	The Harpsicle® Harps Line	9	Bracketing and Placing
4	Learning the Harp Parts	10	Playing Songs
5	Taking Care of Your Harp	11	Changing a String
6	Holding Your Harp	12	Credits

MEL BAY®

1 2 3 4 5 6 7 8 9 0

© 2009 BY MEL BAY PUBLICATIONS, INC., PACIFIC, MO 63069.
ALL RIGHTS RESERVED. INTERNATIONAL COPYRIGHT SECURED. B.M.I. MADE AND PRINTED IN U.S.A.
No part of this publication may be reproduced in whole or in part, or stored in a retrieval system, or transmitted in any form
or by any means, electronic, mechanical, photocopy, recording, or otherwise, without written permission of the publisher.

Visit us on the Web at www.melbay.com — E-mail us at email@melbay.com

Table of Contents

Introduction 3	"Ode to Joy", Joy to the "World" 17
The Harpsicle® Harp 4	"All Through the Night",
Taking Care of Your Harp, Tuning 5	"New World Symphony" 18
Holding Your Harp 6	"Greensleeves" 19
Using Your Hands and Fingers 7	"The Christ Child's Lullaby", "Minuet" 20
Plucking the Strings 8	Changing a String 21
Chords and Arpeggios 9	"Lavender's Blue" 22
Reading Music 10	"Oh, Susanna" 23
Time Signatures and Counting 11	"Gaelic Hymn" 24
Rests, Fingering, Repeat Signs 12	"Au Clair de la Lune" 25
Brackets and Placing, Ties 13	"The Minstrel Boy" 26
Finger Drills 14	"The Waltz of the Rising Sun" 27
"Go Tell Aunt Rhodie", "Yankee Doodle" 15	"To a Wild Rose" 28
"El Primo", Repeats and Endings,	
Dotted Notes, Key Signatures 16	*All songs arranged by Darlene Walton*

About the Author

Darlene Walton has been actively performing music since her first solo at the age of three. Since then, music has been a big part of her life. She studied piano for twelve years, violin and organ for six years, and some guitar thrown in to spice things up. At the age of sixteen she started her church musician career, and has played either piano or organ almost every week since. Darlene has been a piano teacher and choir director for many years, and in 2001 she added harp teacher to her resume.

As part of a gospel group called "Shine", Darlene helped produce and write an album with all original music and lyrics, which the group performed at many venues. More recently Darlene has made two solo harp CDs. *The Harp and the Rising Sun* contains popular tunes and some Celtic music. Her second CD, *Quiet Praise*, features solo harp versions of gospel favorites. Darlene was also featured in a Sentimental Reflections DVD.

At present, Darlene works as the Showroom Manager for Rees Harps Incorporated. She stays busy composing music and rehearsing with her eighteen–piece Harpsicle® Harp choir. She has performed two times at the state of Indiana Inaugurations for Governor Mitch Daniels, plays at the Neo-Natal Intensive Care unit and in the Dialysis unit at a large Cincinnati hospital. She also plays for weddings, dinners, funerals, art shows, festivals, and many other venues. Darlene loves teaching both private and group harp lessons and piano lessons. Taking the stress out of learning to play an instrument is Darlene's greatest gift to her students.

For Darlene Walton the harp has been a major blessing in her life. She says it's a lot more fun than piano and she wishes she had started playing it back in fifth grade when she first fell in love with the harp's beautiful mellow tones.

Chapter 1

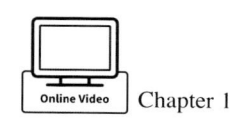

Introduction

This book is a self-teaching, beginning method for the Harpsicle® Harp and other harps both small and large. The teaching and fingering method is largely the same for all harps. The warm mellow tones produced by the Harpsicle® Harp are favored among harp therapists and recommended by harp teachers worldwide as a beginning instrument. The Harpsicle® Harp is also very popular among professionals, for small groups and sessions, and for traveling. Within the spectrum of string instruments the harp is considered one of the easiest for beginners to play. So let's begin!

Access to a companion online video is included with this book. For the most part, the book and the video cover the same material in the same sequence. I highly recommend that you watch the video first and then continue to use it as a reference if needed.

The first part of the book contains important information and instruction about the harp itself, including how to hold the harp, how the hands and fingers are positioned and how they move, tuning your instrument, and other important topics. The last half of the book moves on to playing music. There is a section on reading music. If you already read music you can skip part of that section and move to the area that pertains to harp technique. I have included some familiar pieces of music to get you started.

When this book is successfully completed, there are many other books available for the Harpsicle® Harp and other harps. Remember, always have fun as you learn and you'll have many hours of pleasure as you fall in love with the harp.

Note: If you have a Grand Harpsicle® Harp or a larger harp, the number of strings and size of the instrument will, of course, be different than is outlined in this book. The method and technique for playing your instrument should still apply. Middle C will be in a different place and you will probably have more strings on the low end of your harp.

A special thank you to Melissa Irwin for her drawings and Tawnya Karsteter for her photography.

-Darlene Walton

Look for other solo Harpsicle® Harp music books coming soon from Mel Bay Publications, Inc.

The Harpsicle® Harp

Chapters 2 & 3

Congratulations on choosing the Harpsicle® Harp. You are going to have great fun as you learn to play your new instrument. The companion online video is designed to further explain the information found within the book. Please watch it, and use it along with the book.

If you have chosen a Harpsicle® Harp, it does not have levers and will play songs in the key of C and Am. It may be tuned to any key by using your wrench. There are millions of songs in the key of C, or you can transpose to the key of C or Am. The Sharpsicle™ Harp has C and F levers and can play songs in the keys of C, Am, G, Em, D, and Bm, without retuning. Other levers may be added later if you wish. The Flatsicle™ Harp has C, F, and B levers and can play in the keys of C, Am, G, Em, D, Bm, F, and Dm, without being retuned. If you have a Fullsicle™ Harp or a Grand Harpsicle® Harp it has full levers which can be raised and lowered to play in any key.

The Harp

Chapter 4

Knowing some of the harp parts will be helpful as you learn to tune and play your instrument.

- The neck is the curved part at the top of your harp
- The soundbox is the rectangle hollow box that produces most of the sound. The holes in the back of the soundbox are used as access holes to change strings, insert sound equipment, etc.
- The pillar, or column, is the piece that connects the neck and the soundbox.
- The strings are attached to the silver threaded piano pins, or tuning pins. These pins are turned with your tuning wrench (key) to keep your harp in tune.
- If your harp has levers, it will have bridge pins below the tuning pins. They are used to align the strings.
- The levers are below the bridge pins. The lever is pushed up to raise the tone one half step (tone) to make a sharp.
- The red strings are C and the dark blue strings are F. Even the large symphony harps have the red and blue strings. They are very important in the playing process.
- If you have a Harpsicle® Harp it will have guitar strap buttons at the top and bottom so you can attach a guitar strap and play standing or walking.

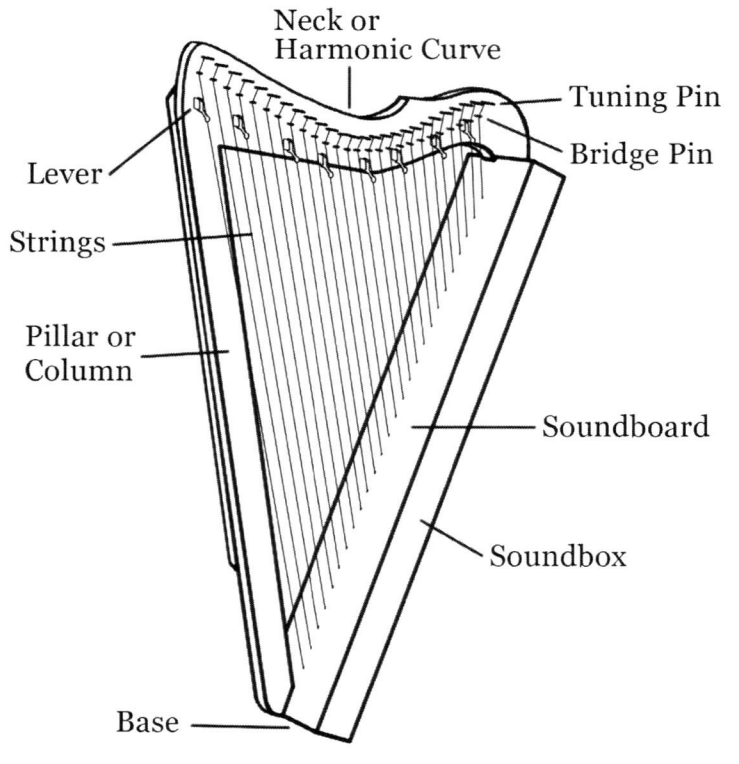

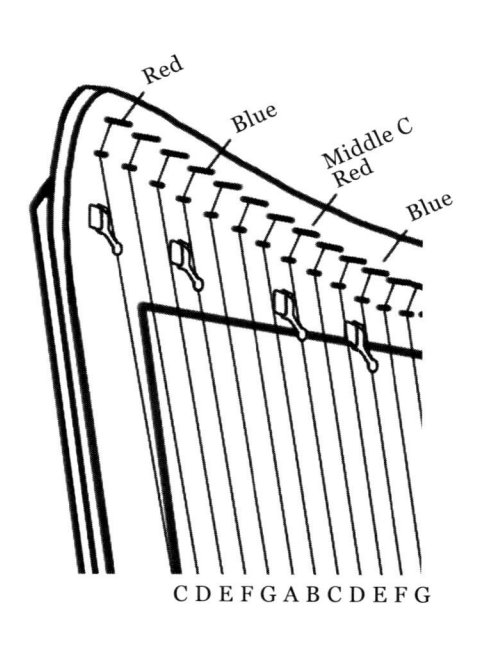

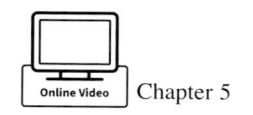

Taking Care of Your Harp

Chapter 5

The Harpsicle® Harp is a low maintenance instrument. Follow these simple instructions.
- Your harp can be stored or displayed on its back, in a Harpsicle® stand, in a harp bag, or hanging by one of its access holes.
- You can dust your harp right along with your furniture. A dusting type product, like Pledge, on a rag is fine. Try not to polish the strings. It can make them slippery or squeaky for a while.
Go to Harpsicle® Harps.com for more information.
- Do not set your harp next to a heat source or by a window that gets sun all day long.
- Leaving your harp in a hot car for an extended amount of time can cause severe damage to the wood or glue.
- Getting your harp wet without drying it immediately can damage the finish.

Tuning

When you first get your harp it will need a lot of tuning, at least once a day. Tuning it twice a day would be better. Even if you don't play it that day, tune it anyway. The more often you tune it the quicker it will hold its tune. The strings have to stretch and the soundbox has to compress and even belly–up a little. This process takes time, so be patient with your new baby. You will be tuning the harp to the do-re-me scale starting with the lowest string and continuing all the way up to the highest string. Use the tuning wrench which is included with your harp. We recommend using an electronic chromatic tuner. Place batteries in the electronic tuner and read the operating instructions that come with the tuner.

1. If you have a lap harp, lay a cloth on the table (to protect the harp) and lay the harp on the cloth with the tuning pins facing up. Place the electronic tuner close to the soundbox of the harp. If you have a tuner pick up clip, attach it to the soundbox hole in the back of the harp.
2. Pluck your lowest string (longest string). If you have a Harpsicle® Harp that string will be a C. The screen and needle on your tuner will show you what note the string is producing. If your harp is out of tune, it may read something other than the correct note. In most cases your harp is going to be flat. If you are tuning a C and the screen reads B, A, or G, the string is too low and you will need to raise the pitch by tightening the string until it reads C. Place your tuning wrench on the C tuning pin and turn it clockwise to tighten the string while lightly plucking the string with your other hand until the tuner reads a C.
3. Now that the tuner reads C, look at the meter. If the needle reads left of center, it means the C is too low (flat) and you need to tighten the string a little. If the needle reads right of the center, the C is too high (sharp) and you need to loosen the string a little until the needle is in the center.
4. Now pluck the next string (the next shortest string) and repeat steps three and four.
5. Repeat the process with the other strings. Make sure you are plucking the same string that you are trying to tune. If you are turning your wrench and nothing is changing on the tuner meter, stop and make sure you are plucking the right string. Tightening the string too much can cause it to break.
6. Tuning the harp for the first few times may take awhile, but after you get accustomed to it you will be tuning your harp in about three minutes or less. Especially with a new harp, it is wise to go through the entire tuning process more than once. You will find that by tuning up all the strings the ones you did first may be flat again because the tightening of the other strings raised the soundboard just enough to reduce the tension of the original strings just slightly. The more frequently you tune the harp the sooner the soundboard will settle in, and then the harp will start to hold tune.
7. Occasionally a string may sound different than the others (buzzing, metallic sound, thumping). This is caused by the string vibrating against its own wrappings on the tuning pin. Simply pull the string away from the wrappings and the string will sound clearly again.

Holding Your Harp

Chapter 6

If you have a Harpsicle® Harp or other lap harp follow these directions: Sit in a comfortable chair, cross your feet at the ankle and place the base of the harp on the upper inside part of your calves. You should not have to squeeze your legs together to hold the harp. The harp should rest in the pit created by crossing your ankles. Lean the top of the soundbox back until the harp rests against your right shoulder. The harp is held the same way for left handed people. The column or pillar should be facing away from you. If your knees are pointing at twelve o'clock, the harp should be pointing away from you at ten or eleven o'clock. This allows you to see the strings easier while keeping your back and neck straight and comfortable.

If you have a floor harp follow these directions: Sit in a comfortable chair with your feet flat on the floor. Your back should be comfortably straight. Place the harp between your knees and lean the harp back until it rests lightly against your right shoulder. If you have a smaller floor harp you might want to use a lower chair or put your harp up on a small stool about six or seven inches high to reach a comfortable height. The column or pillar should be facing away from you. If your knees are pointing at twelve o'clock, the harp should be pointing away from you at ten or eleven o'clock. This allows you to see the strings easier while keeping your back and neck straight and comfortable.

You may find the Harpsicle® Harp stick helpful in holding your lap harp. You should not have to hold the harp with both hands or squeeze your wrists in to help hold the harp. You will need both your hands to be free and play, not to hold the harp. If this is a problem for you, then try a stick.

Below are the directions for inserting the Harpsicle® Harp stick into your harp.

1. Lay a cloth or blanket on a table. Gently lay harp on table with the soundbox slightly hanging over the edge.

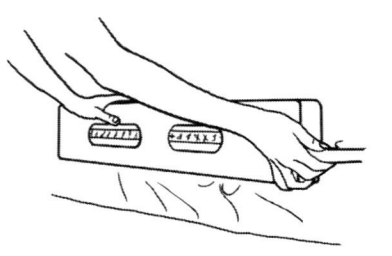

2. Unscrew the wing nut on your Harpsicle® Harp Stick (but do not take wing nut off) and pull apart the two pieces of wood.

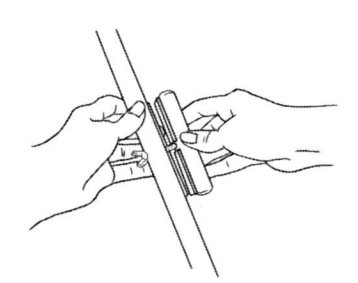

3. Put the smaller piece inside the lower access hole in the soundbox. Be sure the pieces are perpendicular with the harp and tighten the wing nut. If your harp feels unbalanced when holding, loosen the wing nut and move the Harpsicle® Harp Stick up or down until comfortable.

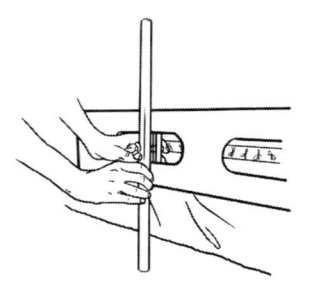

4. Once you have attached your Harpsicle® Harp Stick and your harp feels balanced, lay it across your lap.

Using Your Hands and Fingers

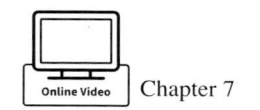

Chapter 7

Using Your Hands and Fingers

One of the best favors you can do for yourself when playing the harp is to pay attention to how you use your hands and fingers. A proper technique will assure you that your playing will be comfortable and pain free. At first you will be concentrating on which finger to use and making sure you are plucking the string properly. It may feel very awkward at first, but soon it will become comfortable. Instead of concentrating on it all the time it will become a habit.

The following picture shows which fingers to use. **Notice the little finger is never used.**

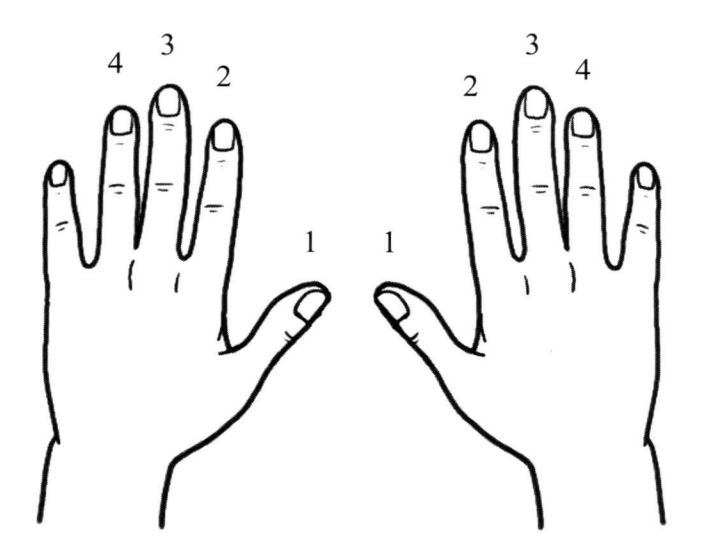

Finger Position
1. Place your hands on either side of the harp and relax them. Keep your wrists straight like you would if you were shaking hands with someone.
2. Keeping your fingers relaxed, raise the thumbs so they are above the fingers. Then turn your hand so that the palms are angled toward the floor. Your thumbs should never go below your fingers. You should be able to see the back of your hand.
3. Place your thumb (#1) on one of the strings so that the **side** of the thumb, next to the nail, contacts the string. Place fingers #2, #3, #4, on each of the next three strings so that the **side** of your fingertips, next to the nail, are on the strings. Using the **side** of your fingertips, and not the ball of your finger, will give you a better tone since there is less flesh on the side of your finger. It will also prevent your fingernails from clacking against the strings.

The picture below shows the correct hand position.

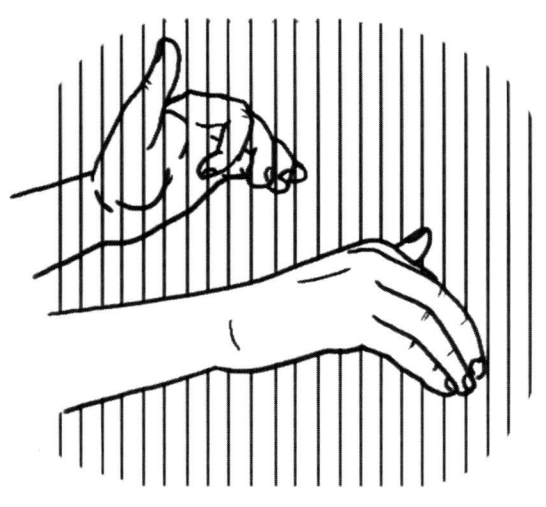

Plucking the Strings

Strings are plucked in the middle of the string or slightly below the middle to obtain the best tone.

1. Place your right hand on the strings as described in the finger position drawing on the previous page. While touching all four strings firmly, pull finger #4 off the string and drop it into your palm. Dropping the finger into the palm will give you the best tone. If you pluck too lightly, you get a weak tone. If you pluck too firmly, you get a buzz or brassy sound from the string instead of a beautiful tone.
2. Now pluck fingers #3 and #2 in the same manner, dropping them into your palm. Swing the finger like a pendulum would swing, parallel to the strings. Do not curl the ends of the fingers when you drop them into your palm.
3. Now pluck the thumb (#1) in the opposite direction away from you, always keeping it above the fingers. The thumb will rest on the middle knuckle of your index finger.
4. Repeat the above steps using your left hand.
5. Spend some time practicing this motion with both hands until it feels comfortable. Remember to relax your hands and shoulders while you play. It's fun isn't it!

Playing a Chord and an Arpeggio

Chapter 8

Playing a chord (or triad) consisting of three notes is a technique you will want to perfect. You will use it regularly, especially in the bass clef with your left hand. An arpeggio is simply a broken chord. A chord or arpeggio is easy to play. It consists of three notes, the first, the third, and the fifth of the octave, in other words every other note. Lets try a C arpeggio with your right hand.

- Place your middle finger (#3) on middle C and leave it there.
- Place your index finger (#2) on E and leave it there.
- Place your thumb (#1) on G.
- First, pluck the C and bring that middle finger back into your palm.
- Now pluck E and bring your finger back into your palm.
- Finally, pluck the G with your thumb and bring it over the middle knuckle of your index finger.
- Now try the same process with your left hand starting on the next C up from middle C.
- If you start at your lowest C and place C chord with your left hand and then place the next C chord with your right hand, you can alternate hands and go all the way up to the top of your harp playing one arpeggio at a time.
- If you want to play an F arpeggio, simply repeat the same steps starting with F then A, C.
- This will work starting with any note. You will always have a chord or an arpeggio.
- If you want to play a chord, place all your fingers as you would for an arpeggio and pluck all the strings at the same time, bringing your fingers into your palm. And your thumb over the middle knuckle.
- You can get a C chord by starting on C, an F chord by starting on F, a G chord by starting on G and so on.
- If you want your chords to sound more like a harp, you should play a roll chord. This is accomplished by using a very fast arpeggio type motion. The notes are almost played together, but not quite. This technique is the most common way to play a chord and is used most of the time unless the piece is fast or calls for a different technique. The roll chord takes practice, so start with arpeggios and chords and work your way up to roll chords. Be patient!

The following page provides some chord and arpeggio practice.

Chords and Arpeggios

Practice these arpeggios and chords first with your right hand, then with your left hand.

NOTE: Bracketing and placing will be discussed in the Reading Music section to follow.

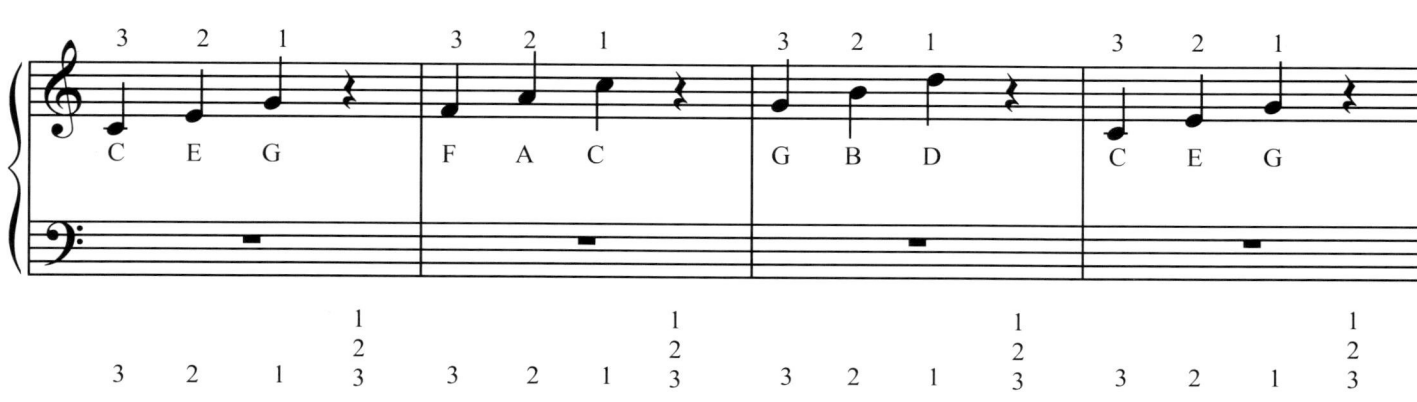

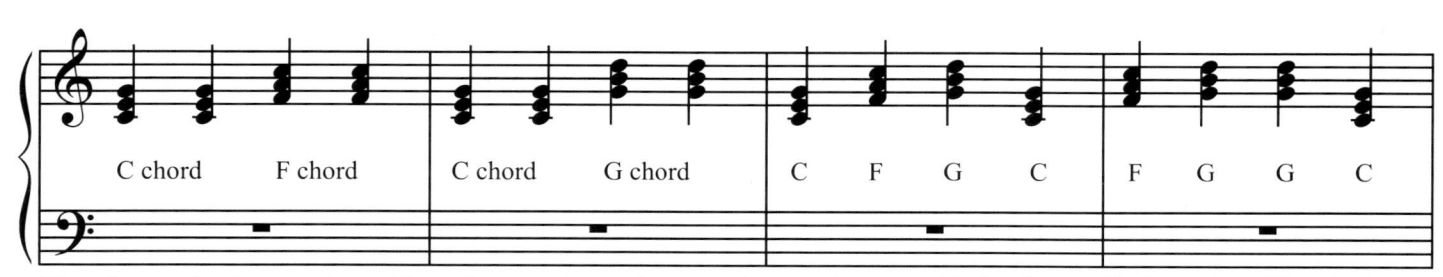

Chords can be inverted, or flipped around, so they can be used more efficiently. A C chord is still a C chord no matter which order the three notes are in. Below are some examples of inversions you may need later on.

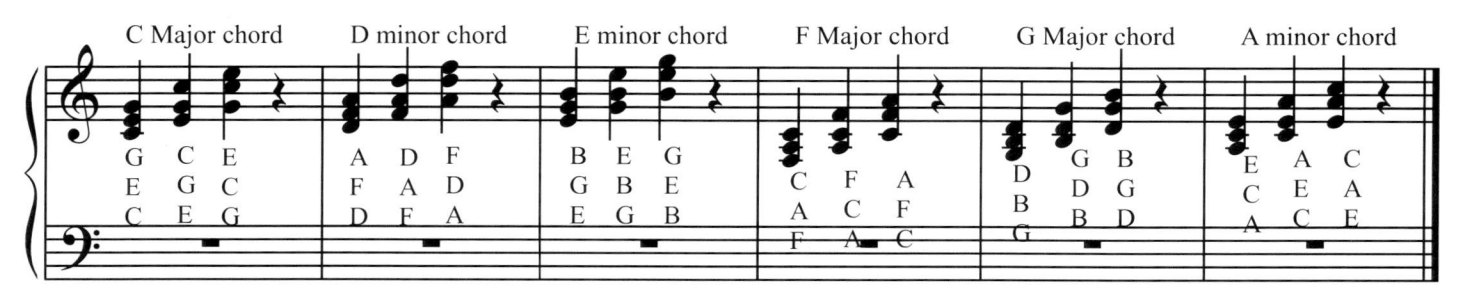

Reading Music

The Grand Staff, pictured below, is joined together by a bracket and contains all the notes. There are five lines and four spaces in each clef. The treble clef (or G clef) is generally played with the right hand. The bass clef or (F clef) is generally played with the left hand. Each note is assigned to each line or space and no other note can occupy that place. The staff is divided into measures and each measure is divided by bar lines. At the end of the song there should be a final double bar line.

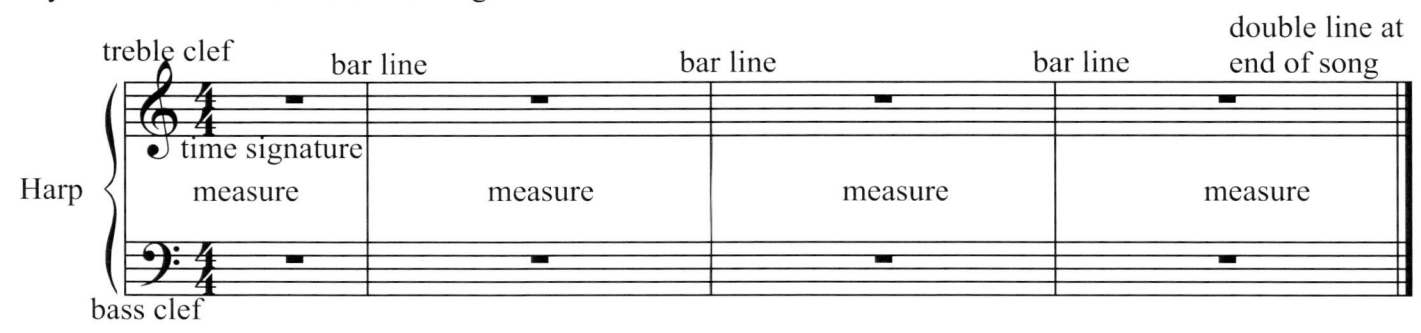

The musical alphabet is from A to G, A, B, C, D, E, F, G, A, B, C, D, etc. All red strings are C and all blue strings are F. Middle C is the second red string from the bottom if you have a Harpsicle® Harp. Below are the strings on your harp starting at the bottom, or the lowest note. The higher the note is on the staff, the higher the pitch and the closer the note is to your body.

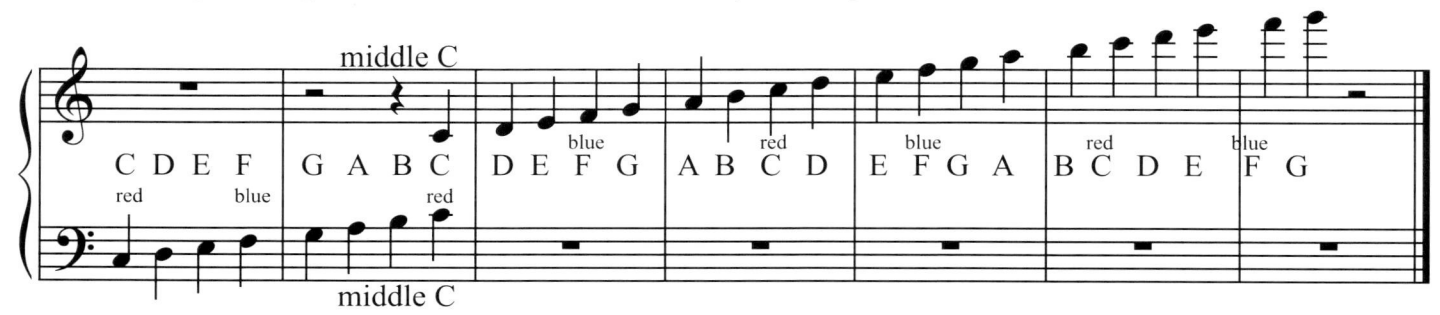

Sometimes the right hand plays below middle C but the notes are still considered treble clef notes. The left hand often plays above middle C as well and those notes are still bass clef notes. I have written those notes on the staff below. The small lines through the notes are called ledger lines.

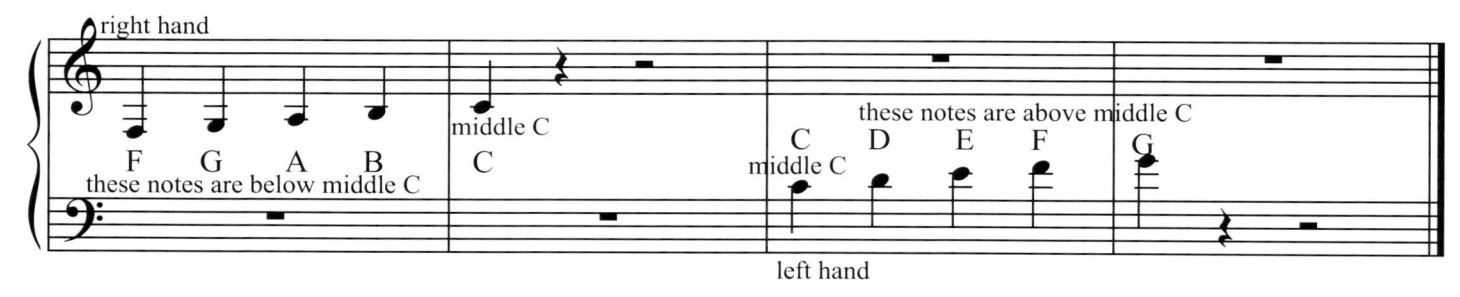

Here are some rhymes to make learning notes easier! Come on, it's not so bad! Each note is the first letter of the word in the rhyme, except for face, of course.

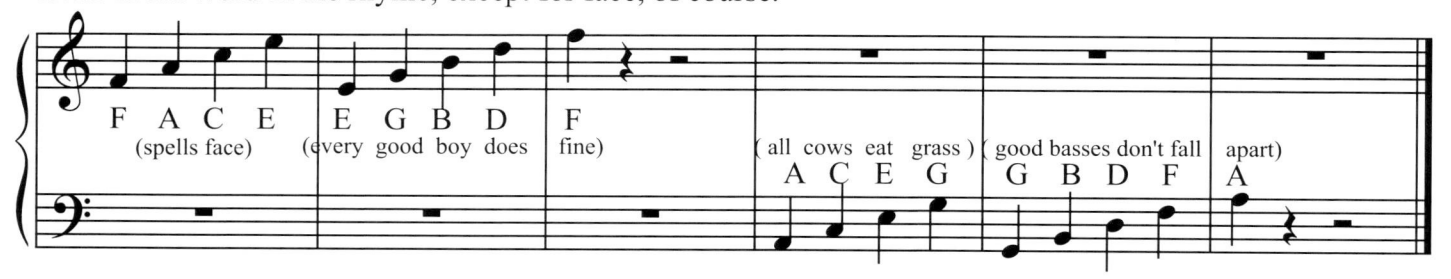

F A C E (spells face)
E G B D F (every good boy does fine)
A C E G (all cows eat grass)
G B D F A (good basses don't fall apart)

Time Signatures and Counting

Time signatures indicate how many counts are in each measure. Below are some common time signatures. The top number tells you how many counts are in each measure. The bottom number indicates what type of note receives one count.

When the bottom number is four it means a quarter note gets one count. When the bottom number is eight it means an eighth note gets one count.

Counting is a very important part in the playing process. This holds true for any instrument. There are several different kinds of notes and each one has its own time value. Below I have described some of the most common notes.

At the beginning of a song you must check the time signature and that will determine how many counts are in each measure. For example, when you have 4/4 time as below you count 1 2 3 4 then start over on the new measure and count 1 2 3 4, etc.

If your time signature is 6/8 time, then you would count 1 2 3 4 5 6 then start over on the next measure and count 1 2 3 4 5 6, etc.

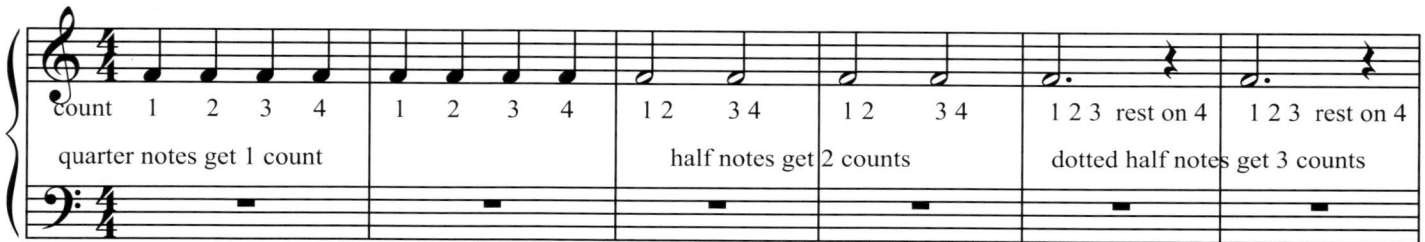

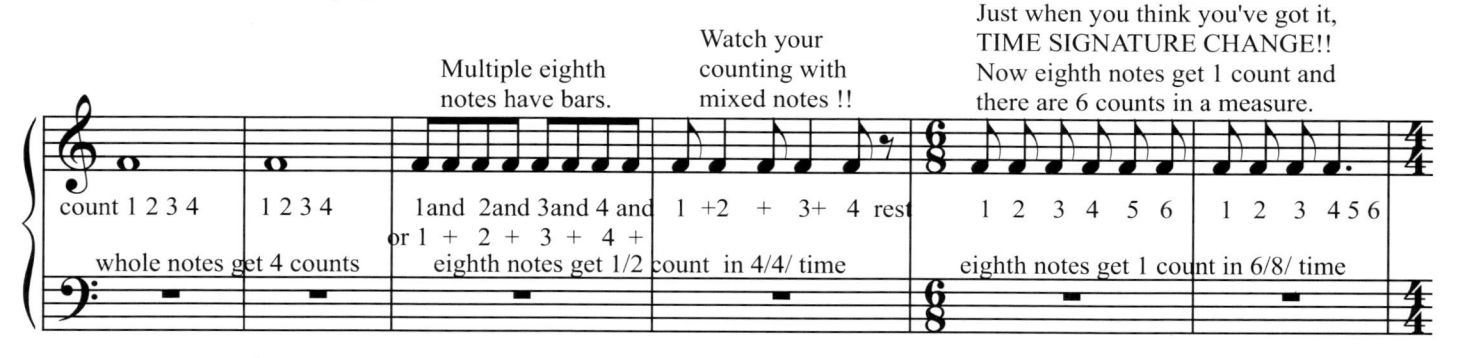

Dotted notes are very common and need to be counted in the following fashion; 1 and 2 and 3 and 4 and, or 1+ 2 +3 + 4+. A dot after a note increases the value of that note by one half its original value. A dotted quarter note is worth one and one half counts. A dotted half note is worth three counts. Counts must equal the top number of the time signature at the end of each measure.

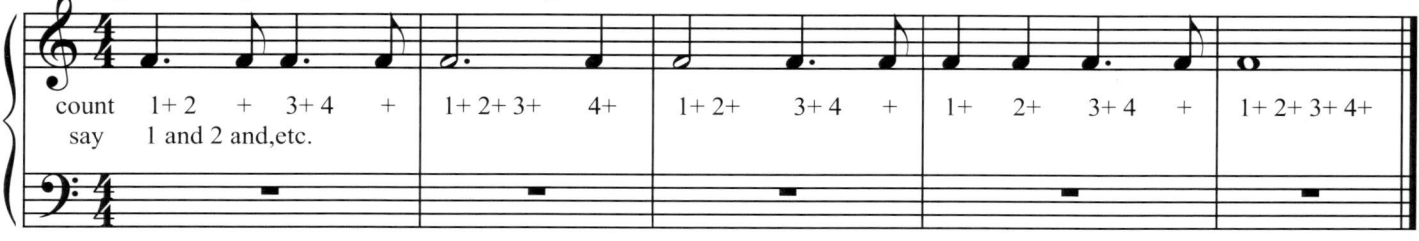

Rests

When your hands are not playing they are resting, and the rests also have time values. Usually one hand or the other will be playing. The rests are combined with notes to achieve the correct count for each measure.

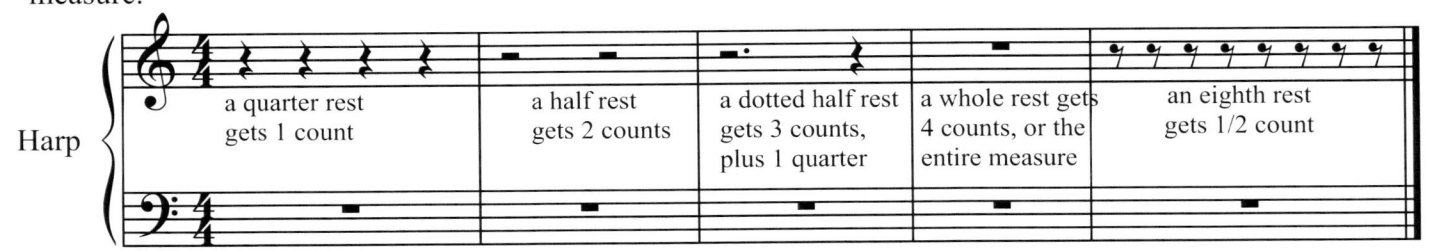

- a quarter rest gets 1 count
- a half rest gets 2 counts
- a dotted half rest gets 3 counts, plus 1 quarter
- a whole rest gets 4 counts, or the entire measure
- an eighth rest gets 1/2 count

Notice the left hand has whole rests in all the measures.

Fingering

As with any other instrument, fingering on the harp is very important. When playing the harp, your thumb is number 1, index finger number 2, middle finger number 3, and ring finger number 4. Your little finger, or pinkie, is never used. Try the line below. I have marked the fingering and the name of the notes for you. The fingering is the same for the right and left hands, unlike the piano where the fingers go in opposite directions.

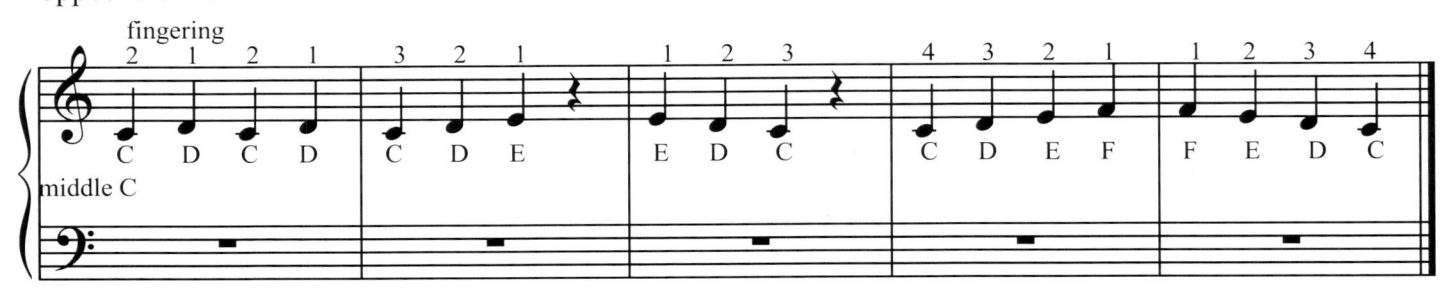

*Remember Middle C is the second red string from the lowest (longest) string.

Try the line below which is written for your left hand in the bass clef.

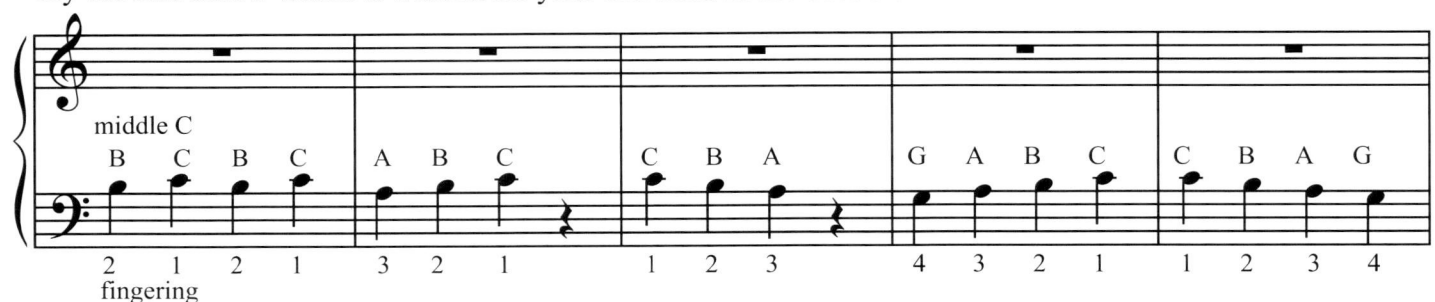

Repeat Signs

The repeat sign means that all, or a portion of the song is to be repeated.

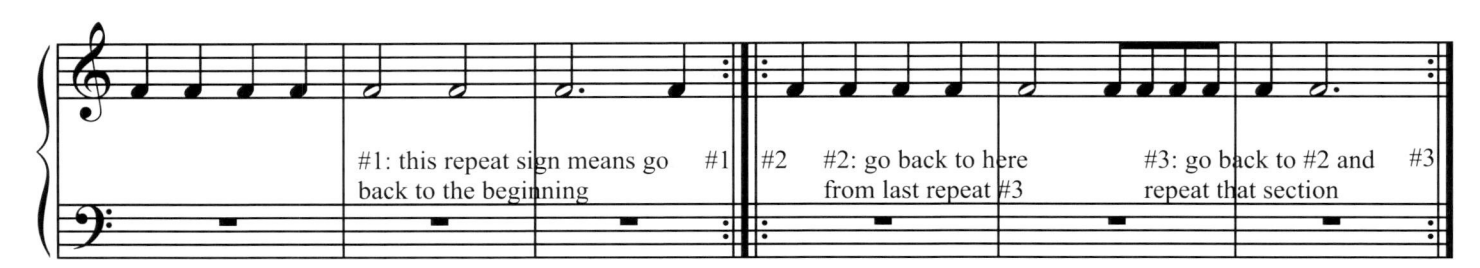

#1: this repeat sign means go back to the beginning

#2: go back to here from last repeat #3

#3: go back to #2 and repeat that section

Brackets and Placing

Bracketing (or placing) is an important part of harp technique. A group (or bracket) of fingers is placed on the strings before you begin to play, and plucked one at a time. Each finger remains placed until it plucks its note. After each finger is played it is dropped down into the palm and is ready to place the next bracket.

Remember it is important to leave the fingers on the strings until they play. After the first finger plays its note, the rest of the fingers are still placed on the strings until it is their turn to play. Then put them away into the palm until the next bracket. When all the fingers are used, you should have a fist without the ends of the fingers curled.

Try the following line using brackets and placing with your right hand. Then try it with your left hand.

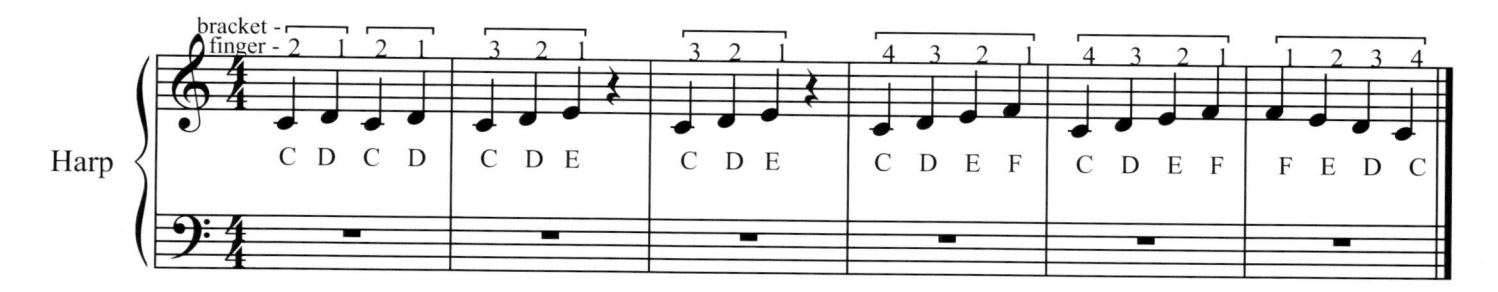

In order to know the location of fingers without having to look at your harp, overlapping brackets are used. Here is how they work. Place the first group of fingers and play as usual until you come to the overlapping bracket. At this point, place the next bracket, play the remaining note on the first bracket, and continue.

Try the following line using overlapping brackets with your right hand and then with your left hand.

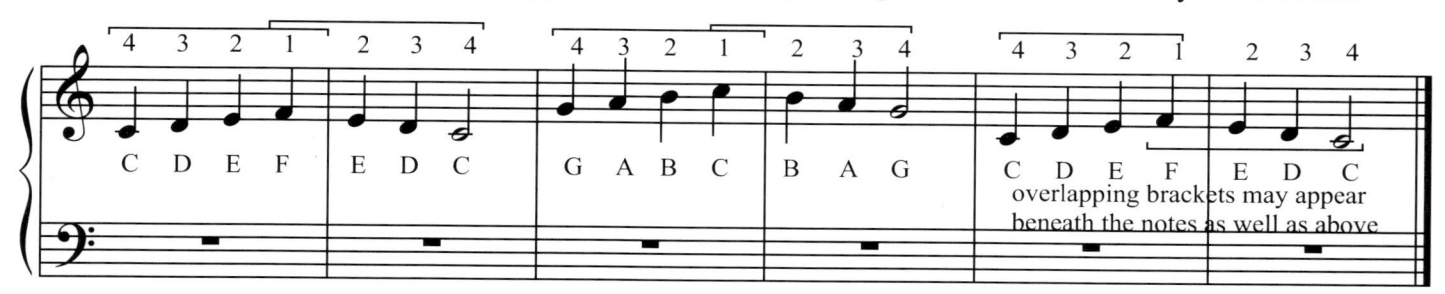

overlapping brackets may appear beneath the notes as well as above

Ties

A tie is a curved line that connects two notes of the same pitch. They must be the same notes to have a tie. Play the first note and count the value of the note. Do not play the second note, but continue to count that note's value before going on with the remainder of the piece.

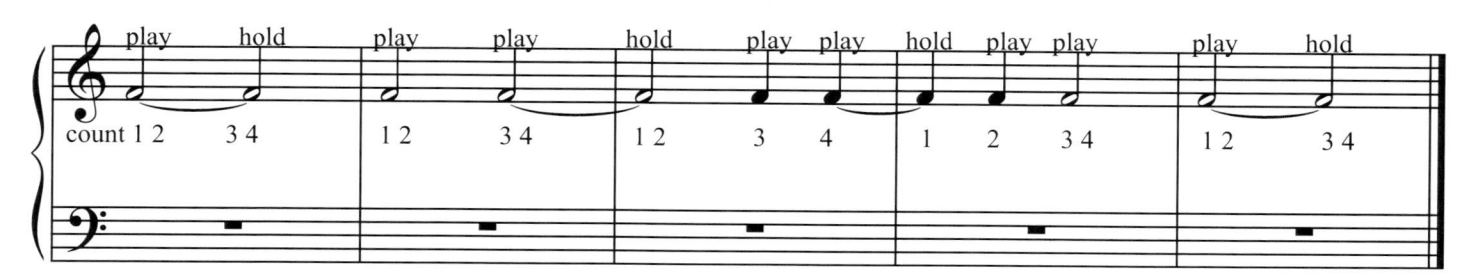

Finger Drills

Try these drills with your right hand alone. Remember to place your fingers as the brackets indicate. Then try the drills with your left hand alone, using the same fingering. When you are comfortable with that, try the drills with both hands together. The left hand will start one octave lower thatn the right, or the C below middle C.

The first line of the finger drills is not mentioned on the Teach Yourself to Play video. The video starts with the second line of these drills.

Go Tell Aunt Rhodie

Chapter 10

This piece is written for the right hand alone, but you can also play it with your left hand just as you did with the finger drills. Notice there are half notes in this piece which get two counts and a whole note at the end which gets four counts. Remember to place!

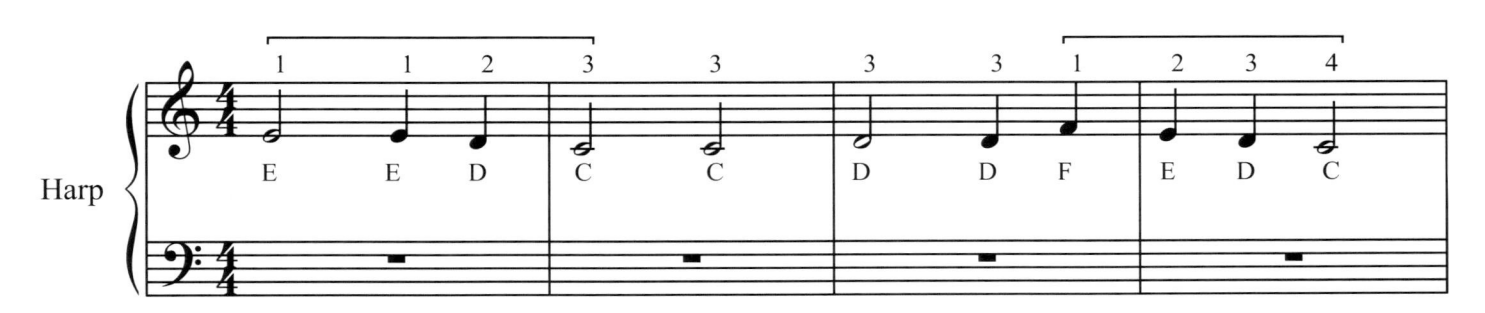

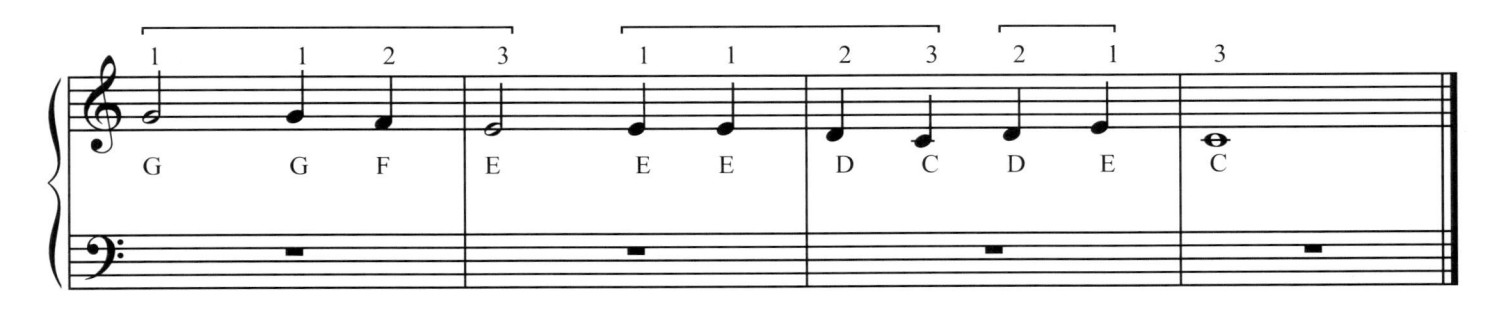

Yankee Doodle

This tune starts one octave up from middle C. Notice the notes are higher on the staff.

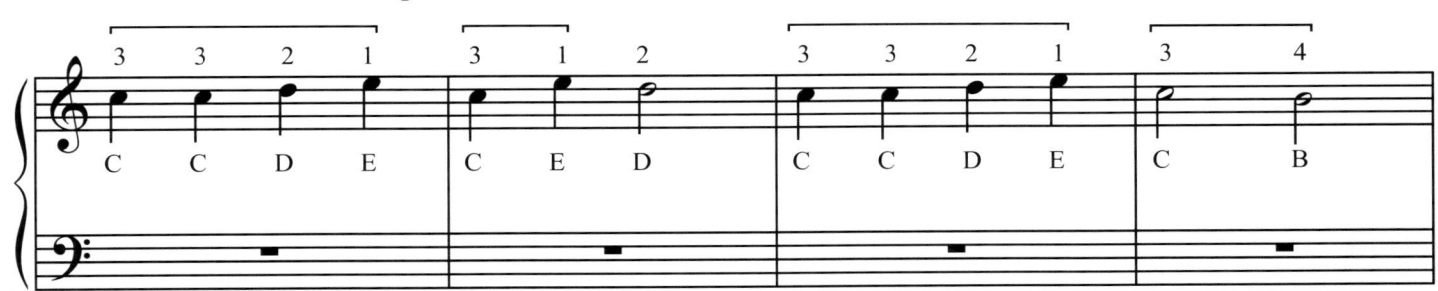

Curved line below indicates a thumb slide. Slide thumb from F to E without raising it from the string.

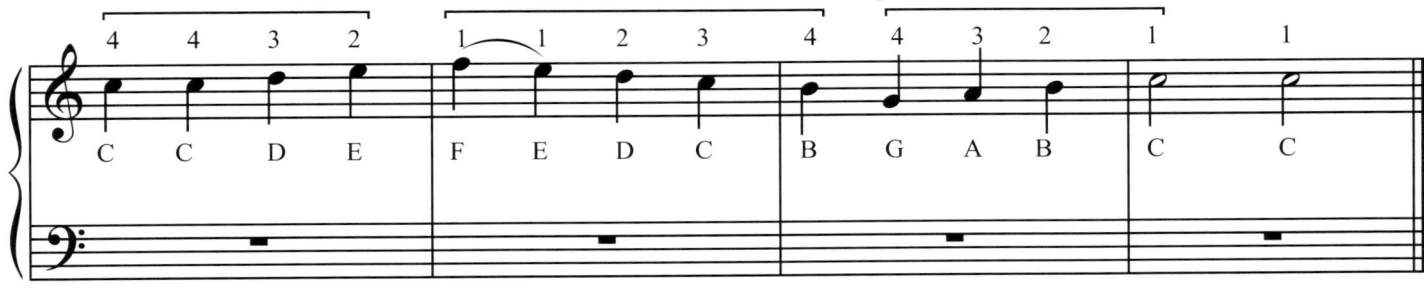

El Primo

The following piece adds some notes for your left hand. Play the left hand note together with the note directly above it. The notes for the left hand are dotted half notes and are held for the entire three counts in the measure. Obviously you can't hold the string like you would hold a piano note. The sound from the plucked string will carry for the three beats.

Repeats and Endings

The next selection on the following page contains a repeat sign at the end of the fourth measure. You learned about the repeat sign in the **Reading Music** section earlier in the book. If you are unsure what to do, go back to page 12 and look at it again.

First and second endings are very common and easy to play. Simply play the first section of the song with the first ending. Then repeat that section and skip the first ending and go to the second ending. You then continue the song as usual. Some pieces contain more than one repeated section, so make sure you look at the piece before you start to play.

Dotted Notes

Dotted notes are very common and are scattered throughout the remaining songs in the book. They simply take a little extra counting, that's all. A dot after a note makes it worth one half more than it was worth. For instance a quarter note is worth one count. A dotted quarter note is worth one and one half counts. Often a dotted quarter note is followed by an eighth note to make the last half of the count(eighth notes are worth one half count). A dotted half note is worth three counts instead of two. Dotted half notes are not used in two four time because there are only two counts in each measure. Counting is discussed in the **Reading Music** section on page 11.

Key Signatures

Harpsicles do not have levers so all the songs in this book are in the key of C or A minor. If your harp has levers, these songs are still fine to play. Just don't use your levers. If a song has sharps in the key signature, then simply flip up the levers according to the key, one sharp, raise F's, two sharps, raise F's and C's, etc. If a song has a B flat, then you will need a lever on the B string. Then raise your B levers and tune as usual, tuning the B to a B natural. Now when you lower the B lever you will have B flat. Leave your B's raised all the time unless youn need a B flat. This same procedure will work for E's and A's. It's called tuning to E flat.

Ode to Joy

Some of the brackets have been removed from sight. From this point forward you should continue to place your fingers before you play.

See below your right hand rests for two counts while your left hand plays the G as melody.

Joy to the World

Remember to place even though the brackets aren't there.

All Through the Night

This piece starts on the C above middle C. It contains dotted notes so count carefully! The last half of the song is played with fingers #1 and #2. The technique is described in the video. It's like twisting the lid off a ketchup bottle with two fingers. Don't forget the repeat.

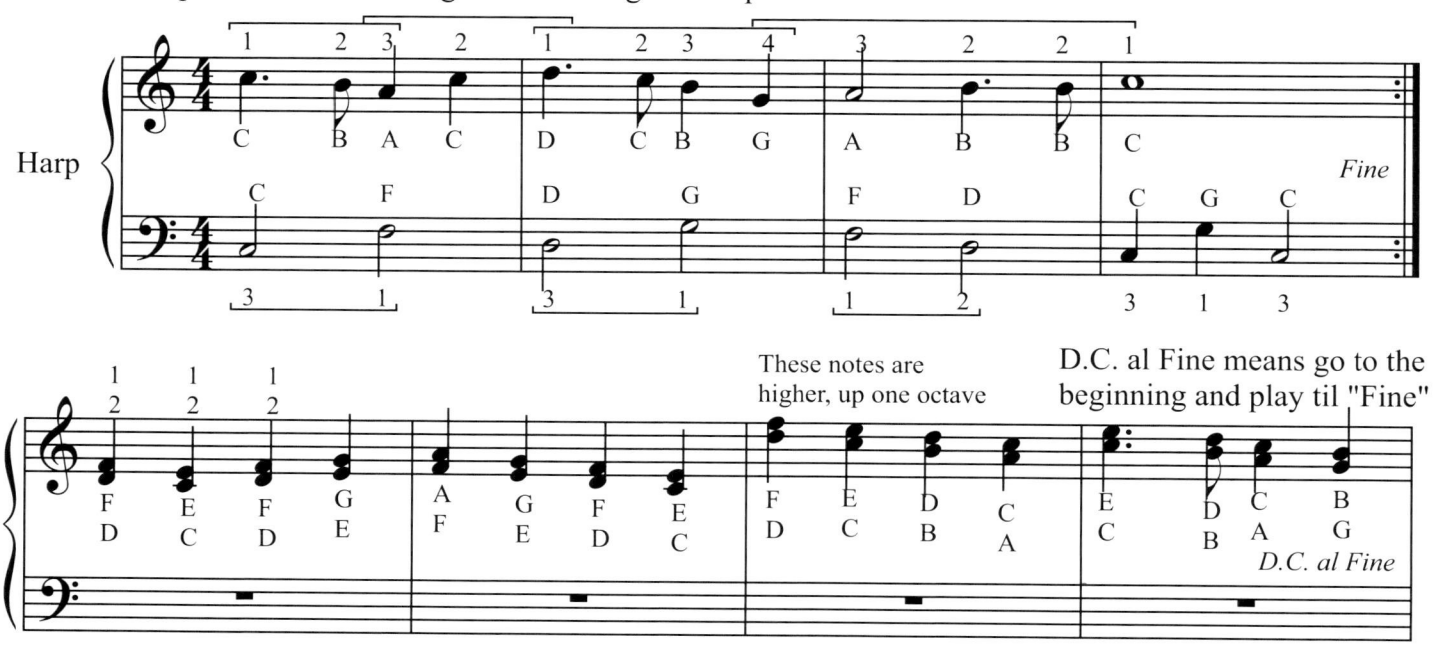

Harp

Measures 1–5 (right hand): C B A C | D C B G | A B B | C — *Fine*
Left hand: C F | D G | F D | C G C
Left hand fingering: 3 1 | 3 1 | 1 2 | 3 1 3

Second line (right hand, "These notes are higher, up one octave"):
F D / E C | F D / G E | A F / G E | F D / E C | F D / E C / D B / C A | E C / D B / C A / B G

D.C. al Fine means go to the beginning and play til "Fine"

D.C. al Fine

New World Symphony

The following selection adds chords to the left hand. Try roll chords for harp effect.

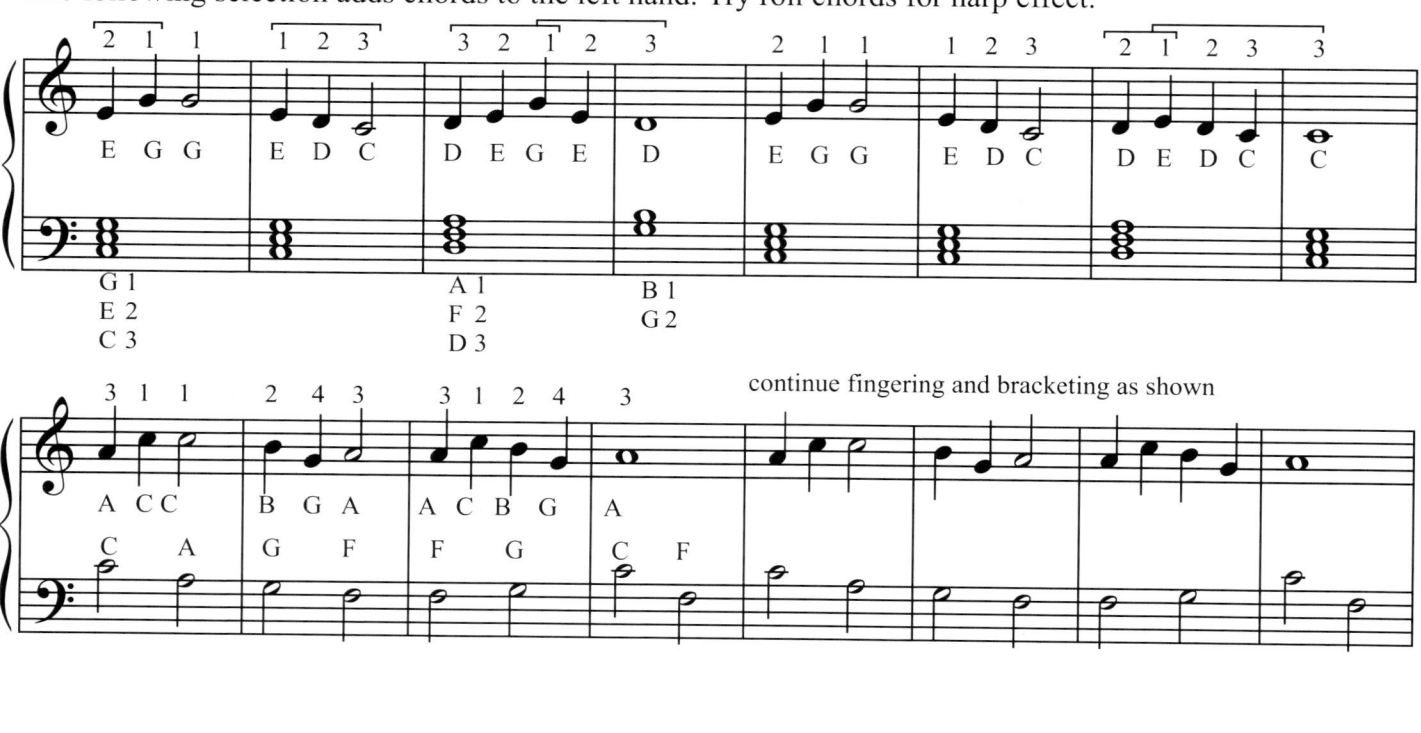

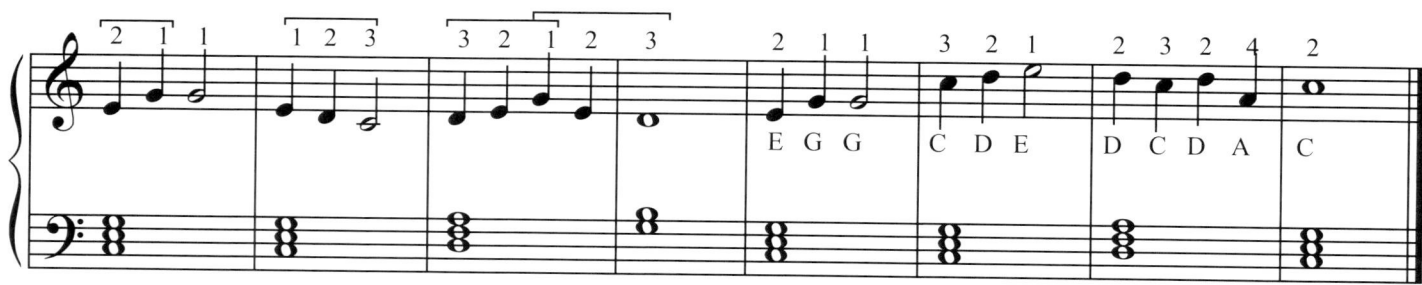

Right hand: E G G | E D C | D E G E | D | E G G | E D C | D E D C | C
Left hand chords:
- C 3 / E 2 / G 1
- D 3 / F 2 / A 1
- G 2 / B 1

Second line: A C C | B G A | A C B G | A | (continue fingering and bracketing as shown)
with inner voices: C A | G F | F G | C F

Third line: (continued) E G G | C D E | D C D A | C

18

Greensleeves

Greensleeves is written with 3 counts in each measure. Watch out for dotted quarter notes. For example the third measure; count the dotted quarter (1 and 2), the next eighth note gets (and), and the last quarter note gets (3 and). The left hand is largely arpeggios. This song is in the key of A minor.

Note: This song starts with a pick up note. It starts on the third count. The end of the song has two counts so it comes out even.

This treble clef G is up one octave. The G above the middle G.

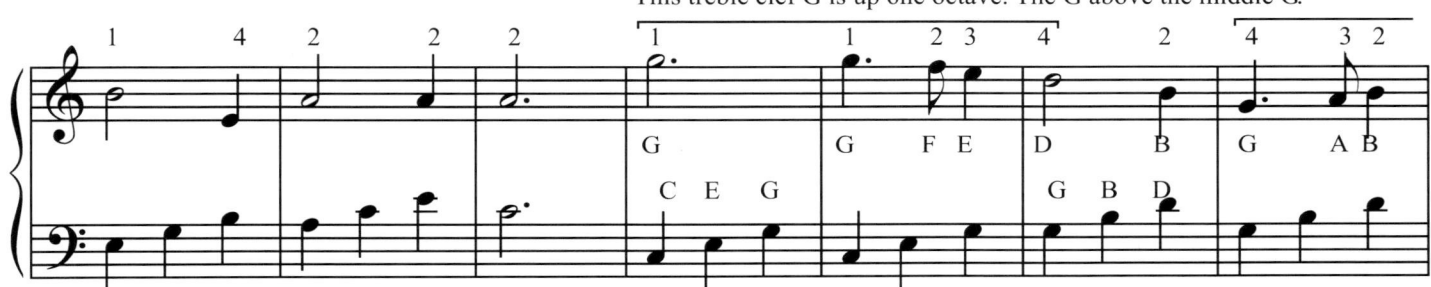

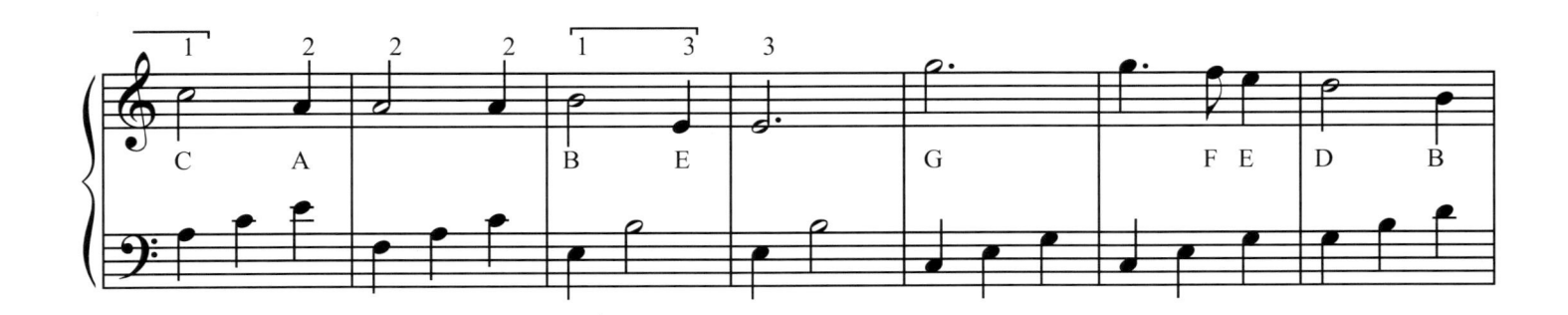

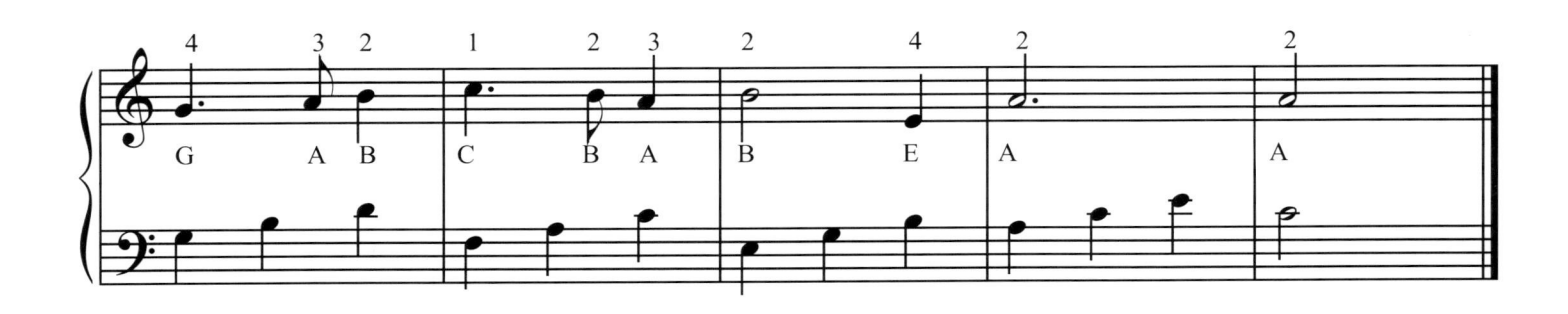

The Christ Child's Lullaby

This piece has a tie at the end. The tie is discussed in the **Reading Music** section on page 13. It also has a repeat at the end. Repeat the entire song.

Minuet

Bach's Minuet is not on the video. It has three counts in each measure. It also has a first and second ending. Play the tune through with the first ending, then play it through with the second ending. Remember eighth notes (with the bars on them) get 1/2 count. Don't forget to place!

J.S. Bach

Changing a String

Chapter 11

So, you broke a string. That's O.K. Strings can break a day after they have been put on, or last a decade or more. The first time you change a string it may seem difficult, but it quickly becomes easier with practice. The following steps will guide you through a string change.

1. Remove all parts of the broken string.
2. Select the proper replacement string. To do this, locate the number of the string that is broken. Count from the shortest string (#1) to the broken string. Then look on the string chart that comes with your harp (or look at the chart below) and select the string according to its number.
3. After selecting the string it is time to install it. Run the string through the string hole of the sound board, pushing it into the soundbox. Reach in the access hole and pull the string out the access hole enough to tie a knot in it. This method is easier than trying to tie the knot first then pushing the string through the hole from the inside. Tie the knot as shown in the diagram below. Be sure to use an extra piece of string or a piece of leather to prevent the knot from being pulled through the hole under string tension. After the knot has been tied, pull the string through and seat the knot firmly against the midrib and soundboard.
4. Now that the knot is seated against the midrib, grab the other end of the string and pull it all the way up to the tuning pin. It is important that you will have at least three wraps around the tuning pin when you are done. To assure three or more wraps, pull the string past the tuning pin and cut the string one and one half to two (1 1/2 to 2) inches past the tuning pin.
5. The Harpsicle® Harp and some other lap harps have microthread tuning pins (usually silver). You need to turn the pin counter clockwise about four full turns before inserting the string into the hole. If you don't, the pin may eventually screw too deeply into the neck. If you have tapered pins (usually black) you do not have to turn the pin before putting on the new string. The tapered pin works somewhat like a cork. If it becomes loose at any time you can wiggle it back and forth while pushing with your tuning wrench, like you would push a cork into a bottle, and the pin should tighten up.
6. Bring the string up to pitch slowly. Turning too quickly may cause the string to break. The new string will go out of tune quickly for a while until it stretches and the knot tightens.

Harpsicle® Harp String Chart

String #	Note	Diameter	Color
1	G	.025	
2	F	.025	blue
3	E	.025	
4	D	.028	
5	C	.028	red
6	B	.028	
7	A	.028	
8	G	.032	
9	F	.032	blue
10	E	.032	
11	D	.032	
12	C	.036	red
13	B	.036	
14	A	.036	
15	G	.036	
16	F	.036	blue
17	E	.040	
18	D	.040	
19	C	.045	red
20	B	.045	
21	A	.045	
22	G	.050	
23	F	.050	blue
24	E	.050	
25	D	.055	
26	C	.060	red

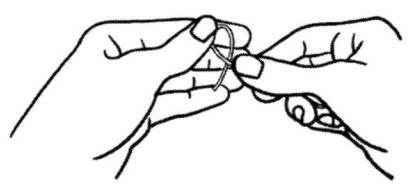

1. First make one loop with the end of your string.

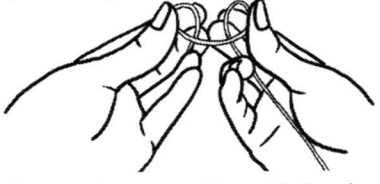

2. Then make a second loop. Notice the ends of the string are behind the loops.

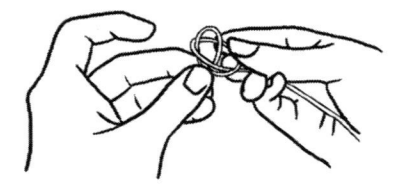

3. Take the second loop you made (on the right side) and put it over the first loop (on the left). The left loop will now be inside the right loop.

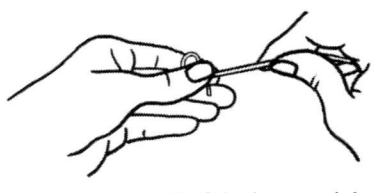

4. Pull the long tail of the knot to tighten and finish your knot.

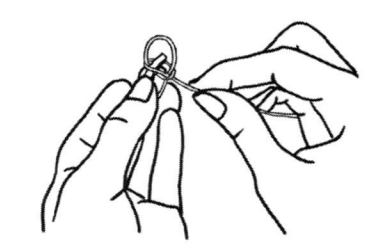

Insert a piece of string or leather to prevent the knot from slipping through the eyelet on the soundboard for extra security for smaller gauged strings.

Lavender's Blue

The following song is not on the video. It has four counts in each measure. Remember the eighth notes (with the bar) get one half count. The whole notes in the treble clef (right hand) at the end of each line get four counts. The brackets are marked, so don't forget to place your fingers on the strings before you start to play

Slowly

Oh, Susanna

This tune is not on the video. It starts with a pick up note on the fourth count. Notice there is a repeat at the end of the second line. Double notes in the third line are played with fingers #1 and #2 on both hands. Some of the labeling of notes and brackets will be left out, intentionally, in order to help you memorize the notes. The finger numbers provided should help you with the placing. If you need help, look back to the **Reading Music** section and review your notes. Remember to have fun while you learn!

Gaelic Hymn

The next selection is not found on the video. I have included chords indicated above the treble clef. The chords can be used to expand your music by adding the full chord with your right or left hand if you wish. The right hand (treble clef) already has a few chords written in the music. The chords should be played with fingers #1, #2, and #3 together. Roll chords should be used if possible. Remember to place even if the brackets aren't there!

Au Clair de la Lune

The following folk song starts one C up from middle C. I have added several chords, since it is a simple melody. I have included the chord indicators above the treble clef. The chord stays the same until you see the next chord indicator. Feel free to add your own chord arrangements to the tune. Practice your roll chords whenever you have three notes together as a chord.

Moderately

The Minstrel Boy

The Minstrel Boy is a beautiful song from Ireland about a young soldier who died in battle with his beloved harp by his side. His last act was to cut his harp strings so his harp could not be played by the enemy. This piece contains dotted quarter notes which get one and one half counts and eighth notes which get one half count. Be careful as you count! Try playing the song up one octave the second time through.

Remember, the higher the note on the staff, the higher the pitch and the closer it is to your body. The lower the note is on the staff, the lower the pitch and the farther it is away from you.

The Waltz of the Rising Sun

This is a simplified version of the title song from my CD. It's a little more challenging than the previous pieces. I suggest you practice the right hand part until you have it mastered, and then move on to the left hand. After both hands are playing well separately, then combine them. The song should be played in a flowing, peaceful manner. Imagine the beauty of the sun as it dances its way above the horizon. This piece has a *D.C. al Fine* at the end, which means go back to the beginning and repeat until you come to *Fine*.

Lightly

Darlene Walton

To a Wild Rose

This well-known classical piece is written with two counts in each measure. Practice each hand separately.

Moderately **Macdowell**